The Late Bloomer
...not your mother's poetry

The Late Bloomer
by C.S. Scotkin
Copyright © 2009 Tangled Web Press

Edited by:
Richard Brotbeck
Elaine S. Polin

Cover Art by:
C.J. Bredeson, © 2009
used with the kind permission of the artist. Artisans Gallery, 1479 S. Belcher Rd.,
Largo FL 33771. www.artisansofflorida.com, cbredeson2@tampabay.rr.com

Cover Layout by:
Richard Brotbeck

The Late Bloomer
Copyright © 2009 Tangled Web Press
ISBN 978-0-578-02757-9

Tangled Web Press
PO Box 233
Shawnee Mission, KS 66201

The Late Bloomer

...not your mother's poetry

INTRODUCTION

TANGLED WEB PRESS was founded in 2007. Our website, POETS OF MARS, was born on January 20th, 2008. The TANGLED WEB INTERNET POETRY CONTEST began on January 1st, 2009. From the beginning, our goal has been to seek out poetic voices within the clamor and chaos of the Internet. We listen and learn and teach and inspire, not with lofty ideals but with actions. We host discussions and workshops, and we post our own poetry for review and critique.

We set this thing in motion two years ago because we felt that the modern American poetic soul was not being fully represented in the collections and award-winning publications available on today's library and bookstore shelves. In our book, OH WHAT A TANGLED WEB, POETRY OF THE INTERNET 2008, we stress that perfect artifice does not always tell the best stories or present the newest and freshest viewpoints.

THE LATE BLOOMER by Cynthia Scotkin, is the second book in our New American Poets Series. Cynthia has been a Licensed Practical Nurse since 1979. Her understanding of humanity speaks clearly in her poetry. The ideas have been swirling around inside her head for decades. She has only recently decided to organize them into modern poetry.

We love her work. It is our dearest wish that you will soon feel the same way. It is up to her, the poet, to engage the reader. You will be her art critic.

Richard Brotbeck

FOREWORD

Cynthia Scotkin is a "late bloomer" in the sense that her flower is only now being seen in the garden of modern American literature. Poetry has been a part of her life for years. The Internet, and POETS OF MARS in particular, is where her poetic voice has grown louder.

It has been my pleasure to watch her poetry develop over the last two years. She eagerly absorbs the sights and sounds of life and spins her stories in delicate language that soothes, suggests, and sometime alarms.

In THE LATE BLOOMER she explores the adult mind and soul in many diverse poetic forms. A lover of the English Sonnet, she strives to master the form. In addition to the metrical styles, her free form poetry also sings to the reader with its many universal themes: poems about kids and cats, classical themes, self exploration, love and loss, as well as miscellaneous musings and fun poems.

The emotions in her verse are genuine. An LPN since 1979, and the mother of twin boys, this transplanted New Englander has made the South her home. The flavors of both sugar cane and bitter herbs accent her literary brew.

This is a book for people of all ages. Once you read THE LATE BLOOMER, your childhood love of poetry will arise again.

Elaine S. Polin

A NOTE FROM THE POET

Writing poetry was not a childhood dream of mine. I write nursing notes for the greater part of the day.

A friend suggested I look at poetry on the Internet, so I gave it a try. I read for a while, then tried to write a poem. That poem was quite forgettable, but it did introduce me to the POETS OF MARS.

I learned that writing poetry is more difficult, and much more fun than I had ever imagined. Poems, good and not so good (and a few dreadful) came pouring out.

I have written over 400 since that first one in July 2008. Now, writing poetry seems to be more like eating potato chips...

There are so many people to thank: My friends, my family, both immediate and extended, my colleagues at Fusion Health Care, the English teachers from 40 years ago, my mother and grandmother who gave me their love of reading.

I especially want to thank Richard Brotbeck (T.D. Euwaite) for suggesting this project, Elaine Polin for her encouragement and editorial skills, and all the other POETS OF MARS and Earth for their support.

Cynthia S. Scotkin

This book is dedicated to David and Tyler,
Rolf, Jenny and Emery.

Great Diana

SISYPHUS' DAUGHTER

I wish to say a word about my sight
Small gift to bards and troubadours who see
Some glimpse of wisdom or of words' delight
A lover's song from shadow's edge sung sweet.
I stand outside the yard where poets play
Their games with words and metaphors for all
Within this maze I cannot find my way
Nor stile with which to climb its heady wall.
In earnest now this process has begun.
My mind, a seedling, will it have a bud
To nurture, water, open to the sun
Or drown in tears, words trampled in the mud?
I hope and trust the words I write today
Might have some worth to you along the way.

AUTUMN ROADS

I drive too fast on Autumn roads
and think I know them well.
Falling leaves of memory
impede my forward view.
Windblown, mind swirling
backlit by blinding rays of
sunset, recollection.

I wonder if these hues are true,
will they manifest in moonlight
as I rush ever onward
over these final hills
toward home?

VIRTUALLY REAL?

Here virtual, reality are blurred.
A dream when sleep
ensnares me in its net.
Images from Morpheus,
force fed
And in my head
the movie comes alive.

I meet you all
and yet I know you not.
Your smiles embrace each other
through the mist.
A list of names
now matched with each new face.
Your voices
so familiar to my ears.

This thought now comes
to haunt me through the day.
How do you see me
writing at my desk?
The best of images
I can display?
Would my reality
upturn your day?

EVENSONG

Let me
sit in the quiet
breathe life
release the day
let it float
away on exhaled
emotion.

Let me
melt into cool
darkness
blur my
borders until
I cannot tell
where I end
and Eternity
begins.

POETRY

Hold your breath as words, those shooting stars
fall ever closer to your mind
white hot signal flares for all
these streaking brilliant ones
flashing through our minds
explode old thoughts
with beauty
and new
truth.

JACKSON POLLOCK

The film is old,
grainy.
An old barn
where Pollock freed
canvas from easel,
banished convention.

His paint swirls,
crawls, leaps
explodes
from above,
meaninglessness,
lines and drips, motion
becoming.

Coherent progression
chaotic order
subatomic universes.
A map,
his mortal brain
daring to stare through
Divine Creativity.

HARRY

The Sun's coming up
A big orange ball
I'm calling him Harry
instead of Sol.

As Harry shines bright
This great ball of gas
breaks up the night
dark falls on the grass.

Harry, aflame, glides
through a blue sky
looks down on the Earth
a great laughing eye.

OAK

These great Oak limbs
reach out to snare a cloud
to bathe her leaves
in soft and lighter wet,
and dry in morning light;
winds sing their praise
while rushing through
the smaller branches' net.

The little ones
who live upon her breast
or in her crown
lack not for food or shade.
Protected in her shadowed
roots, they rest, while storms
fling out their jagged,
white hot blades.

She silent stands and guards
through darkest night;
this tow'ring mother watches over me,
a witness to her strength
and my delight, my garden's diadem
this old oak tree.

GREAT DIANA

Great Diana
from Cynthos' height
full draped in
gauzy, misted light
stares at mortals
through the night.

She pulls her bow
as mortals scheme,
Her arrow flies,
Olympian beam,
through the dark,
bestows a dream.

BURNISHED GOLD

So if indeed there is a God
God sneaks around my soul
my soul has fingerprints, all smudged
all smudged with burnished gold.

Gold wings of cherubim fly through
fly through unseeing eyes
eyes searching for another place
another place, sans cries.

Cries from the multitudes swell loud,
swell loud to gain God's ear
God's ear? Could it be really true
True words assuaging fear?

Fear nothing searching for your heart
your heart and soul divine
divine with fingerprints all smudged
smudged, burnished gold, like mine.

CERES

Who now remembers Ceres' rites of old
When grains and fruits were from her bosom brought?
Full rev'rent children knew the prayers and told
of Goddess' love, Her mercy ever sought.
Great sheaves of wheat, gold corn adorn Her hair.
Her throne now fallow at the Harvest Moon,
And hurry we to Harvest Home so fair
Prepare Her gifts' return, Her rightful boon.
This small green doll of woven silk and shuck
I bury in this decimated plot
To sleep away the winter's harder luck,
To resurrect in Spring, forget me not.
When once we lived in Ceres' strong embrace
Were we a less forgetful selfish race?

SUN CYCLES

We say the Sun does rise, the Sun does set,
illusion for our eyes which cannot see
I wish that I could stand so far away
to see the Earth's great dance of stately grace.
For as the Sun sets here I know full well
that elsewhere it is rising proud and strong
and brings its light and warmth to others who
shall wait through their long nights, eyes looking East.
We know the Earth is round, our home in space
turns on its axis as we round the Sun.
it tilts, and as we see the seasons come
We know this race of life has one less lap.

I know now why the ancient ones did chant
and sacrifice to bring back new, the day.

THE LADY AND THE CARPENTER

Your calloused fingers learned my face today
Such gentleness belies your daily task
My lips so traced have no clear words to say
My breathing holds the question, dare I ask?
You find my hands, slow raise them to your lips
Bestow a kiss unhurried, each in turn.
I flee o'er rocks, I fear that I may slip.
My thoughts most carnal, make my face to burn.
I run from you, yet my heart yearns to stay
Your humble dwelling seems a paradise.
Our diff'rences, will they come into play?
Or have the Fates conspired this surprise?
I'll run with longing back into your arms
To build with you a home safe from all harms.

A MEMORY

Scratchy Old Spice hugs
brush cut steel
stogie scented love
mixed in rose essence
a garden long ago
where Grampa
cut a bloom for me.

LIGHT

I
Sit here
Pen in hand
Aware of light
Too bright for my words
What can express splendor
Nature's love poured on my head
As chrism on the heads of kings
Light bestowed to all who search for truth
Then tell their travelers' tales and visions here.

EXPECTATIONS

I had expectations,
in my soul, a rift.
I'm much wiser now.
When nothing is expected
everything is gift.

Afternoon Delight

MYTHIC SPRING

She calls her lover, Spring wind hears her plea
And dances 'neath budding trees in nuptial rite
To wake the Mother lost in winter's sleep
Inanna lies and waits for Dumazi.
He comes to her, his shepherd staff he bears
And by her leave and love he enters in,
To quicken all Earth's life that she would share,
Her children never knew the weight of sin.
From oldest times these tales which come to us
In deeper places sleep, yet yearn to wake,
Impart Earth's cycled wisdom won, and thus
They toiled in seasons, watched, their voices spake
I ask of you, shall we not learn to see
These ancient myths still speak to such as we.

HEIGHTS

I feared heights.
Climbing mountains
had no charm
for me, looking down,
needing toeholds.

I trembled at
arching bridges
spanning the
openness of hope,
seeing instead
uncertainty's feared abyss.

Each dawn
whispered loudly,
Look up,
your feet know how to walk
higher places,
emancipate your eyes,
gaze beyond horizons.

AFTERNOON DELIGHT?

I had driven way back home
after a very long day
yearned for soup, sandwich and tea
with the cats then, I would play.

I started to make the tuna and soup
Oh yes, I opened a tin.
Crockery crashes, cats yowl,
I rush out, what is this din?

A lamp is smashed to smithereens!
my silk plants, three, all shredded,
my books are scattered on the floor,
you see where this is headed?

Clean up this messy disaster,
two little kitties have fled,
I think it might have been better,
I should have gone straight to bed!

But soon my library's tidy,
I'm feeling quite hungry now,
I head off straight to the kitchen
hear little kitties meow.

I heat chicken soup on the stove
cats on the porch, I utter,
those naughties ate all my tuna,
where is the peanut butter?

A SONNET TO SHAKESPEARE

O Will, I love thy bright acerbic pen,
When thou didst scribe the "Taming of the Shrew"
Didst thou forsee or think a future when
Thy greatest form, a poet might eschew?
Which angel plucked quills from his great wing
So thou couldst pen the words of Juliette?
Yea, all thy words hath made our souls to sing
Near five hundred years, we feel them yet.
For all thy tragedies, thy comedies
For histories that speaketh honour still
Applause now echoes far beyond those seas
And works of Shakespeare maketh theaters fill.
For thy plays and verse eternal liveth
I thank them, for wisdom sure they giveth.

SPRING

Pale gold
pollen hangs,
laughs away
gravity's pull.

Trees full
bloomed white,
barely green
budding leaves.

Infectious spring
I am stricken
with life.

PIXIE WINGS

Under my bed I have a box
with shiny pixie wings
this pretty box is wrapped in gold,
tied up with silver strings.

What can we do with pixie wings?
come close, I'll give a clue!
we can pretend to fly up high
in clouds, just me and you!

Fly over trees and oceans blue
fly over cities, farms
fly over rivers and little brooks
you'll show me all their charms!

And when our flying time is done
when we need to rest
will you please tell us a story
of sights you loved the best?

The pixies who flew with shiny wings
carefully put them away,
hoped they would have a little girl
like you some happy day.

And on a happy day in Spring,
when the flowers were bright and new,
Daddy and Mama got their wish
and she was lovely you!

LITTLE BOY RED
(for Rolf and David)

Little boy red,
Little boy blue
I wonder how
nature knew
you were destined to be one?

Nature divides
splits, surprises.
from one, now two
love divided
multiplies, and there you were...

Alike as two
can ever be
you were yourselves,
oh yes, completely
right from the beginning.

Not even parents
can understand
this bond, entire.
Unseen, real band
holding you together.

Identically
so different,
you always have been
you always will be
our two only children.

A LULLABY FOR EMMY

Look upon this baby's face.
See our miracle of life?
See the truth of love and grace.
Look upon this baby's face.

Look at trusting, wond'ring eyes,
hold her close with loving arms.
No fears now can cloud her skies.
Look at trusting, wond'ring eyes.

See her promise shining bright?
May she live in peaceful times,
As we rock this child tonight.
See her promise shining bright!

The Failure of Love

SCORNED

What metaphor can
keen this pain and grief?
What simile compare
with one soul's cry?
I look for dawn's pure light
but there is none
yet see the sun,
it shines there, in the sky.

My eyes are drought,
a sandy desert waste.
the seeds of love's forgiveness
dry and gone.
Replaced with arctic
numbness in this heart,
my ears are stopped
from hearing any song.

The Earth still turns,
the seasons yet will march
and doors again will open
wide for me.
But not tonight,
I think upon your guile
and lips that dripped
your words' duplicity.

VIXEN

Standing on the Arctic Sea
Where all is cold and white
A vixen shivers, quiv'ring ears
Waits dawning, pure daylight.
She has followed Polar Bear
All through the six-month night
Respectful distance did she keep
On Bear scraps she would bite.
Spring is coming, sea ice cracks
Days lengthen with Sun's might
Voles in meadows green will run
For her kits' appetite.

RELEASE

Hot and bitter tears,
never acidic enough
to dissolve these
old chipped jail bars
I noticed recently.

Always staring through
the emptiness between.
Never hearing my captor self
call my name,
declare my pardon.

Only now with fingers
still death-gripping bars,
I step back as this
hated door swings
…open.

Terrified, I stare
at possibilities,
walk through with
fearful joy.
With amateur courage
I accept release.

FOG

Silence veils
this walk,
senses denied,
falling in this
ephemeral river
flowing upstream
to join with other
haunting shades.
Conspirators
kidnap
the dawn.

SAUL AND ROSE

I met my wife when we were five,
the old man said to me,
I scarce believe we're still alive
this good age, ninety-three.

She was my best friend from the start,
this feeling never wavered
then I proposed when I was six,
A "yes" to me she favored.

We fin'lly wed at twenty-eight,
there was little money,
and I had studied medicine
to support my Honey!

See the picture on the shelf?
That was our wedding day,
we vowed that hour to never part,
and together we would stay.

Oh, yes, we had some times so rough
our baby twins, they died.
Sweet little girls lived but an hour,
my Rose and I still cry.

Then three fine boys were born to us,
they grew up proud and bright
good dads and husbands, all of them,
they're blessings in our sight.

His Rose, who can no longer speak,
her hand put on his knee,
her dark brown eyes spoke love so loud
they nearly deafened me.

He leaned over to kiss her face,
I swear to God above,
I saw those little six year olds
again, they pledged their love.

THE FAILURE OF LOVE

Today I found that pretty golden ring
Ring that graced my finger for so long
Long days and nights it took for me to know
To know, with you, I never could go on.

On looking back, I wonder what I saw
What I saw then clear, when love was new
New seeds of love that fell along the path
The path I walked on, egg shells that you strew.

You strew demands and insults in my heart
My heart and mind could not get through your mask
Your mask, all intellect and ego-struck,
And ego-struck, you weren't up to the task.

The task of marriage soon became too much
Too much, the pain and tears we both have borne,
We both have borne the failure of love,
The failure of love is what I mourn.

DREAMS

I stumbled aimless through my forest
Forest of dreams all weird
Weird, these strange unconscious musings
Musings embraced, yet feared.

Feared faces mix with scary times
Times from my years long past
Long past the time, release these dreams
Dreams vanish, sleep at last.

At last the dreamless sleep I yearned
I yearned for rest complete
Complete and safe in dark night's hand
Night's hand caresses sweet.

Sweet dreams arise like soft gray fog
Gray fog, my waking mind
My waking mind slides silent, back
Back down to dreams divine.

Faulty Vision

DECEPTION

Dandelion fluff words
float, warm breaths
find a field neglected.

Softly fall to root
this empty, nettle stung
heart with promise.

Spring green joyful,
hopeful buds, now
fool's gold blossoms.

Deception's bitter sap
flows in weeds...
gone to seed in other fields.

NIGHTMARE

See ghosts, their trains of icy mist do drag
Lost souls into the mire and dank blight.
Hear loosened cries of harridan and hag,
Hear screams of banshees echo through the night.
Black shadows of vampires across the moon
Make my warm blood to chill within the vein.
My spirit prays for brightness, yearns for noon
As demons circle, dance within my brain!
And bats emerge from blackness in a cave
To fly with devil wings into my face
I shudder in this dream, I am not brave;
My screams are silenced, terror takes their place.
I flail and fight to free myself from sleep
Old depths, subconscious, why these horrors keep?

DESCENT

Iron rusted
memories
bear down,

sorrow's crown
squeezing
thoughts
good and sane
now a void

avoiding
tears

fill
the void's
gaping maw
with aging
rage...

and wait
for blessed release.

SUNDRESS

I know you think this dress is plain, too simple in its cut,
you say the color's cool and clear, yet in your voice a "but,"
I found the fabric in a shop, a shelf hid out of sight
wrapped in old, soft muslin, its shield from dust and light.

Warp and weft in subtle meld I did not see at first,
in color that refreshed my eyes as water quenches thirst.
The lady at the counter smiled, how much would I buy?
I thought that I might take it all, not knowing how I'd cry.

While searching for perfection, many shops did I explore—
Wand'ring aisles, frustrated, till I could search no more.
A vision fashioned in my mind for how this dress must look
I came to understand there was no pattern in a book.

It took long years to craft this dress I wear in day's full sun,
Can ever you appreciate the sewing that I've done?
This simple dress is perfect for my years and for my size
Now I can recognize myself, when mirrors catch my eyes.

A MARTIAN DORSIMBRA

On Mars' great ruddy face, a Golden Dome
With windows bright from many candles lit
Does call to us; this our ancestral home
Becomes a shoe that can no longer fit.

Others went before us, you know,
The Pioneers, they blazed a trail,
Bradbury, Burroughs, Heinlein, Lewis, Bova.
And little roving reporters NASA sent.

And so we come supplied with all our gear
Our hopes and spirits glow forever bright,
The arid waste will soon be terraformed
On Mars' great ruddy face, a Golden Dome.

PRINCESS ROYAL—AN EMMY POEM

She stares with widened eyes and pallor'd cheek,
a Princess Royal, the favored one so fair
and blessed of the Gods with spirit meek
that few refuse her even if they'd dare.
And locked, her padded throne a refuge not
from great discomfort as she seeks escape
the footsteps quick'ning pace does match her heart
unstops her maiden screams, unstops her fate.
Resists a great assault with all her might
and wonder how her armor could be strong
a buckler, girded round and shield full bright
protect this Royal Princess from the Wrong.
The King has come and said unto his Queen
Our Princess does not seem to like green beans.

IF I COULD BE AN APPLE TREE
(for Tyler)

If I could be an apple tree
it would be such a joy
providing rosy goodness
for every girl and boy.

In Spring my blossoms would call bees
with petals, coat the ground
fertilized with buzzful care
I'd grow my fruit all round.

In summer you would see my fruit
from green turn into red
and in the chilly days of Fall
be plucked, you would be fed.

And when the winter snow blows cold
I'd shut down for a while
and dream my apple dreams wherein
sweet blossoms made you smile.

A SPACEY TIME POEM

Dr. Albert Einstein said
Ride a light beam in your head.
Something strange will happen.

(You might want flight insurance)!

Are you up and belted in?
It would be a real sin
To fall, upon the blast-off!

(You see what I mean about flight insurance)!

Now at cosmos' great speed limit
Whoa! Hold on! Now wait a minute!
Something strange does happen.

(I don't think I can get my money back)!

When you see me coming through
What you see is very blue
When you see me go I'm red.

(Don't blame me, talk to Edwin Hubble)!

This little fact, it fills my head
Not without a little dread
I return, you may be dead.

(...wait, just a thought experiment)!
(whew)!

LAMENT OF AN AGING NOVICE

A child will learn to crawl before he walks
And falls shall come with bruises on the knees
But practice daily with desire so great
Success eventual shall come to him.
To write, to play at poetry is fun!
Yet much of what I scribe has little worth
True talent needs true study for the mind
Which disciplines the hand to hold the pen.
I know this truth, no prodigy am I,
Yet I can learn from all the words I write,
The taste of metaphor and simile,
And read all Masters old up to the new.

Shall I not be more diligent and learn
There's more to poetry, not only heart?

A TECH POEM

How do I love Thee, G.P.S.?
Upon this I do ponder.
I love Thee for the length and breadth
of cities where I wander.
In dulcet tones you guide me,
yet never scold nor chide me.
Great bliss and chills of ecstasy!
No longer challenged directionally!
Sweet fruit of our technological tree
greater than gold, your worth to me.

FAULTY VISION

Never thought I'd crave the night
Night full dark with shadows veiled
Veiled from any source of light
Light which makes my vision pale.

Never thought I'd fear the sun
Sun has ever been my source
Source for warmth but now the one
One that has become my cross.

White hot scalding photons burn
Burn and bore through eye and head
Eye and head have not yet learned
Learned that photons are hot lead.

Painful blurred yet I write still
Still I know the price I'll pay
Pay with ice packs and with pill
With pill to sleep the night away.

INDEX

www.ingramcontent.com/pod-product-compliance
Lightning Source LLC
LaVergne TN
LVHW041209080426
835508LV00008B/866